Butterflies
Up Close

Greg Pyers

Chicago, Illinois

© 2005 Raintree

Published by Raintree, a division of Reed Elsevier, Inc.

Chicago, Illinois

Customer Service 888-363-4266

Visit our website at www.raintreelibrary.com

For information, address the publisher: Raintree, 100 N. LaSalle, Suite 1200, Chicago, IL 60602

09 08 07 06 05
10 9 8 7 6 5 4 3 2 1

Printed and bound in Hong Kong and China by South China Printing Company Ltd.

Library of Congress Cataloging-in-Publication Data

Pyers, Greg.
  Butterflies up close / Greg Pyers.
    p. cm. -- (Minibeasts up close)
  Includes bibliographical references and index.
  ISBN 1-4109-1528-X (hc) -- ISBN 1-4109-1535-2 (pb)
  1. Butterflies--Juvenile literature. I. Title. II. Series.

QL544.2.P94 2005
595.78'9--dc22

2004022288

Acknowledgments
The publisher would like to thank the following for permission to reproduce photographs:
Auscape/Kathie Atkinson: pp. **11**, **21**, /Pascal Goetgheluck: p. **12**, /Francois Gilson-Bios: p. **6**, /Brett Gregory: p. **5**, /OSF/Bob Parks: p. **9**, /OSF/Alastair Shay: p. **16**; /Fritz Polking: p. **26**, /John Shaw: p. **14**, /Anne & Jacques Six: pp. **10**, **13**; Lochman Transparencies/Hans & Judy Beste: pp. **20**, **22**, /John Kleczkowski: p. **25**, /Jiri Lochman: p. **4**, /Peter Marsack: pp. **23**, **24**; photolibrary.com: pp. **7**, **27**, **28**; /SPL/Alfred Pasieka: p. **17**; Viridans Images/Mike Coupar: p. **29**; © Paul Zborowski: p. **15**.

Cover photograph of an old world swallowtail butterfly reproduced with permission of Auscape/OSF/Bob Parks.

Every effort has been made to contact copyright holders of any material reproduced in this book. Any omissions will be rectified in subsequent printings if notice is given to the publisher.

Contents

Any words appearing in bold, **like this,** are explained in the Glossary.

Amazing Butterflies!

How many kinds of butterflies have you seen? What colors were their wings and bodies? Were their wings rounded, or shaped like triangles? When you look at them up close, butterflies really are amazing animals.

There are about 20,000 **species**, or kinds, of butterflies in the world.

What are butterflies?

Butterflies are insects. Insects have six legs and no bones inside their bodies. Instead, their bodies have a hard, waterproof skin. This skin is called an **exoskeleton**. Butterflies have four wings.

Butterflies have two separate stages in their lives. The colorful insect that flies from flower to flower is the adult stage. Butterflies exist in an entirely different form early in life. They hatch as caterpillars from eggs laid by female butterflies. Caterpillars crawl among plants and eat leaves.

This caterpillar will one day become a butterfly.

5

Where Do Butterflies Live?

Butterflies are found in many different parts of the world. They live in mountains and cold regions, in dry deserts, and in wetlands. They also live in towns and cities. The **habitats** with the most butterfly **species** are tropical rain forests. These habitats are warm and have plenty of food.

The world's largest butterfly is the female Queen Alexandra's birdwing butterfly. It lives in the rain forests of Papua New Guinea. It measures 11 inches (28 centimeters) across.

Food and warmth

Butterflies feed on **nectar**. This is a sweet liquid inside flowers.

Butterflies like sunny places where there are lots of flowers. Butterflies from cold parts of the world are often dark-colored. Dark colors warm up quicker than light colors.

Apollo butterflies live high in the mountains, where it is cold. Their bodies are covered with fur to help them stay warm.

Caterpillar food

Butterflies grow from caterpillars. Caterpillars eat leaves, not nectar. So, butterflies must live in places that have the right kinds of leaves for their caterpillars.

7

Butterfly Body Parts

A butterfly's body has three main parts. These are the head, the **thorax,** and the **abdomen.** All butterflies have four large wings.

The head

The head has two feelers, called **antennae,** two eyes, and a mouthpart called a **proboscis.** Each antenna is long and thin.

The thorax

The thorax is where the butterfly's wings and legs are attached. There are strong muscles in the thorax. Butterflies need these muscles to flap their large wings.

The abdomen

The abdomen is usually quite narrow. In females, eggs are produced in the abdomen.

Size and shape

Butterflies come in many different sizes and shapes. The smallest butterflies are no bigger than a postage stamp. The largest are wider than an outstretched hand. Some **species** have long, thin wings. Others have short, wide wings. The wings of some species have long tails.

antenna

eye

head

proboscis

wing

leg

thorax

abdomen

Mouthparts and Eating

Butterflies drink **nectar.** Nectar is a high-energy food because it has sugar in it. A butterfly needs plenty of energy to fly.

Some plants have many flowers with lots of nectar. Many butterflies visit these plants. Butterflies also drink juice from ripe fruit and **sap** from plants.

This cabbage white butterfly is drinking nectar through its proboscis.

proboscis

Drinking

A butterfly has no jaws so it cannot eat **solid** food. Its sucks **liquid** through a hollow tube called the **proboscis.** It works like a drinking straw. To drink, the butterfly dips the end of its proboscis into the nectar.

When a butterfly is not drinking, it rolls up its proboscis under its head.

Drinking water

In hot climates, butterflies sometimes gather on wet ground to lap up water. The water is rich in **minerals** that nectar does not contain.

11

Eyes and Seeing

A butterfly's sight helps it to find flowers. It also helps male butterflies find a mate. Butterflies are quite short-sighted, which means that they cannot see very far.

Compound eyes

A butterfly has two large **compound eyes.** Each compound eye is made up of about 6,000 very small eyes. Each small eye faces in a slightly different direction. Together, these small eyes give the butterfly an excellent view to the front, side, and back.

A butterfly's compound eyes are good for clearly seeing movements. They cannot, however, see faraway objects.

In this close-up photo you can see the butterfly's compound eye.

Colors

A butterfly sees different colors from those we see. A flower that looks yellow to us may look blue to a butterfly. The butterfly may also see patterns on the flower surface that we cannot see. These patterns help to show a butterfly where the **nectar** is.

False eyes

Many butterflies have two large spots on their wings. These spots protect the butterflies from birds that might eat them. To a bird, the spots look like eyes. The bird sees the spots and is frightened away, instead of eating the butterfly.

Antennae and Sensing

A butterfly has two feelers called **antennae** on its head. The antennae are used to **sense** the world around it. Smells that float through the air are picked up by the antennae. The smell of **nectar** or fruit tells the butterfly where to fly to find food.

Antennae are also used to find mates. A male flaps his wings to send smells from his wings into the air. A female that is ready to **mate** senses these smells with her antennae.

This cabbage white butterfly is using its antennae to smell a flower.

Feet

A butterfly also senses with its feet. When a butterfly lands on a flower, its feet can help find nectar.

Caterpillars hatch from eggs that a female butterfly lays. The butterfly lays the eggs on plants that the caterpillars can eat. The butterfly uses her feet to find these plants.

Other butterfly senses

A butterfly may use its antennae to touch its mate. Its antennae also pick up changes in wind direction. Butterflies do not have good hearing. They sense **vibrations** made by animals moving near them.

This birdwing butterfly can sense vibrations with its feet.

Wings and Flying

Butterflies have four wings, all attached to the **thorax.** Strong muscles inside the thorax move the butterfly's wings up and down.

Flying

Butterflies beat their wings quite slowly. Some **species** can even glide with just a few flaps now and then. The front edge of each wing is stiff. This helps the wing slice through the air. The rest of the wing is like a sail, helping to push the air aside. This keeps the butterfly in the air.

This European swallowtail is flying between flowers.

Scales

Butterflies cannot fly unless their bodies are quite warm. Their flight muscles will not work if they are cool. To warm up, butterflies lie in a sunny place, with their wings held open. The scales that cover each wing take in heat quickly.

Wing veins

Butterfly wings have thick **veins** running through them. Veins are tubes that carry blood through the wings. Veins also give the wings strength.

This close-up photo shows the scales on a butterfly's wing.

Inside a Butterfly

Butterflies have blood that is clear and a heart that is shaped like a tube.

Blood

A butterfly's blood moves through the spaces in its body. It travels from the head, through the **thorax,** and into the **abdomen.** From there, the butterfly's heart pumps it forward again.

How do butterflies get air?

A butterfly gets air through tiny holes called **spiracles.** There are about ten spiracles down each side of a butterfly's body.

What happens to food?

When a butterfly drinks **nectar,** the liquid moves down to the butterfly's stomach. It is then broken down to release **nutrients.** A butterfly needs nutrients to stay alive. Butterflies do not produce droppings because they do not eat **solid** food.

The brain

A butterfly's brain gets information that it senses through its **antennae,** eyes, and feet. It sends messages to the rest of the body about what to do.

brain

heart

stomach

From Egg to Caterpillar

A female butterfly lays her eggs on plants. In some **species**, the females fly along and let the eggs drop. In other species, the female places groups of eggs on the undersides of leaves. There they are hidden from **predators.**

Caterpillars

Most butterfly eggs hatch a few days after being laid. The eggs of some species may go through winter before hatching in spring. When the eggs do hatch, tiny caterpillars come out. This is called the larval stage. Almost immediately, the caterpillars begin eating.

This glasswing butterfly is laying her eggs on a leaf.

Host plants

Different species of caterpillars eat different plants. The plants they eat are called host plants. Caterpillars of the peacock butterfly eat nettle leaves. This is why a peacock butterfly lays her eggs on nettle bushes. Caterpillars of the common brown butterfly of Australia eat any kind of grass. So this butterfly drops her eggs as she flies over a field.

Meat-eating caterpillars

Harvester butterfly caterpillars of the United States eat insects called woolly aphids. The female lays her eggs among these aphids.

This wanderer butterfly caterpillar is hatching from an egg.

The Life of a Caterpillar

Caterpillars seem to do little else but eat. A caterpillar may eat more than three times its own body weight in a day.

A caterpillar body

A caterpillar body has thirteen parts. It has six legs near its head and several legs called **prolegs** along its body. The legs and prolegs move the caterpillar and help it hold onto leaves as it feeds. A caterpillar has two eyes, but these can only see light and dark.

A caterpillar's jaws need to be strong because leaves are tough to chew.

A strange disguise

The orchard swallowtail caterpillar looks like a bird dropping, and birds leave it alone.

Staying alive

Caterpillars cannot flee from **predators.** They have other ways of avoiding being eaten. Some have a body color that blends with the surroundings. Others have bright colors that warn birds of a nasty taste. Some have bristles and others are poisonous. Some caterpillars are so small that they go into leaves and eat them from the inside. In this way, they can hide from predators.

The bright colors of this birdwing caterpillar warn birds to leave it alone.

A New Butterfly

Caterpillars grow fast. They get too big for their skins and have to **molt.** This means that they shed their skin and grow new, bigger skin. Caterpillars molt several times. After a few weeks of eating and growing, they are ready to become butterflies.

Chrysalis

Changing from a caterpillar into a butterfly is called **metamorphosis.** This begins when a caterpillar attaches itself to a branch. It then sheds its skin for the last time. It is now a **chrysalis.** The skin of the chrysalis hardens. Inside, the caterpillar's body parts break down. They turn into wings, eyes, **antennae,** and other body parts.

This imperial white caterpillar is shedding its skin and becoming a chrysalis.

A butterfly forms

When the butterfly is ready, the chrysalis cracks and the butterfly crawls out. It pumps blood into its wings to stretch them. The butterfly lets the sun dry its body and harden its **exoskeleton.** In a few hours it is ready to fly.

The wings of this young wanderer butterfly will soon stretch and be ready for flight.

Migrating Butterflies

Some butterflies travel, or **migrate,** great distances. The monarch butterfly flies the farthest of all.

Flying south

Every fall, millions of monarchs in North America gather in huge groups called **swarms.** They have drunk plenty of **nectar** and to get ready for the long flight. The swarms fly south to Mexico, California, and Florida, where the weather is warm. They may travel about 1,900 miles (3,000 kilometers) in just a few weeks. The monarch swarms settle on trees and sleep through the winter.

Thousands of monarch butterflies gather in the mountains of Mexico during winter.

Monarch life span

Monarch butterflies can live for eight or nine months.

Flying north

In spring, the monarchs wake and feed on nectar. This will be fuel for the long return flight north. As they travel, the monarchs **mate** and the females lay their eggs on milkweed plants. These are the plants the monarch caterpillars eat.

A monarch caterpillar uses silk to attach itself to a plant. Soon it will become a **chrysalis**.

An Australian migrant

The brown awl butterflies of Queensland, Australia, migrate more than 620 miles (1,000 kilometers) south in early summer. They produce their young and fly north by late summer.

27

Butterflies and Us

Gardeners often use plants that butterflies eat. These plants have lots of **nectar** in their flowers. Gardeners also grow the plants that caterpillars eat so that more butterflies will appear. But some butterflies are not so welcome.

Pests

The caterpillars of the large white butterfly eat cabbage leaves. There are other caterpillars that eat fruit tree leaves. These caterpillars, and the butterflies they turn into, are often sprayed with **insecticide** to kill them.

Most butterflies are harmless and do not damage plants.

Endangered butterflies

Butterfly collecting was very popular in the 1800s. Millions of butterflies were caught, killed, and pinned to boards. But these butterflies would probably have laid their eggs already, and would have died soon anyway. The reason some butterflies are **endangered** today is because their **habitats** have been destroyed.

Butterfly at risk

The Eltham copper (right) is an endangered Australian butterfly. Its caterpillar eats only the leaves of the sweet bursaria bush. In some places, these bushes have been cleared to make way for houses. This is why this butterfly is endangered.

Find Out for Yourself

You are most likely to see butterflies on warm, still days. In a garden, butterflies are most often attracted to blue, purple, white, or yellow flowers growing in sheltered, sunny positions. You may see caterpillars eating a plant. The caterpillars may become the butterflies you like to see in your garden.

Books to read

Braun, Eric, and Sandra Donovan. *Animals of the Rain Forest: Butterflies*. Chicago: Raintree, 2001.

Hibbert, Clare. *The Life of a Butterfly*. Chicago: Raintree, 2004.

Kalman, Bobbie, and Margaret Amy Reiach. *The Life Cycle of a Butterfly*. New York: Crabtree, 2001.

Preston-Mafham, Rod. *Butterflies and Moths*. Chicago: Raintree: 2002.

Schaefer, Lola M. *Butterflies: Pollinators and Nectar-Sippers*. Mankato, Minn.: Capstone, 2001.

Using the Internet

Explore the Internet to find out more about butterflies. Have an adult help you use a search engine. Type in a keyword such as *butterfly*, or the name of a particular butterfly **species.**

Glossary

abdomen   last of the three main sections of an insect

antenna   (more than one are called antennae) feeler on an insect's head

chrysalis   stage in a butterfly's life cycle between caterpillar and adult

compound eye   eye made up of many parts

endangered   at risk of becoming extinct

exoskeleton   hard outside skin of an insect

habitat   place where an animal lives

insecticide   poison that kills insects

mate   when a male and a female come together to produce young

metamorphosis   changes inside a chrysalis from caterpillar to adult

migrate   move from one place to another, often over a long distance

mineral   solid chemical element or compound that occurs in nature in a crystal form

molt   when a growing insect splits open its outside skin and climbs out of it. Many insects need to molt so they can grow.

nectar   sweet liquid inside flowers

nutrient   part of food that is important for an animal's health

predator   animal that kills and eats other animals

proboscis   long tube on a butterfly's mouth that is used for drinking

proleg   leg that extends from the last section of a caterpillar

sap   juice inside a plant

sense   how an animal knows what is going on around it, such as by seeing, smelling, or hearing

solid   hard, not runny

species   type or kind of animal

spiracle   tiny air hole

swarm   many insects moving together

thorax   chest part of an insect

vein   small tube in the body that carries blood

vibration   fast shaking movement

Index